Praise for *Goat, Goddess, Moon*

"*Goat, Goddess, Moon* lovingly traces a lineage through history, myth and new experience. 'I speak broken Greek. We say fluent Greek,' Strisik writes. 'Say it. Say. While standing/ on your head: the Greek alphabet.' These poems—part tender probe of heritage and part ancestral elegy—revel in sumptuous food, the body and the sea. With its nourishing glimpses of identity this collection will encourage any reader to more closely embrace their own cultural inheritance."

— Lauren Camp, New Mexico State Poet Laureate (2022-2025), author of *In Old Sky*

"In *Goat, Goddess, Moon*, Catherine Strisik returns us to the villages and rituals of a Greece where time is marked by what's passed down, in anecdotes, recipes, and the ways particular Greek words like *psomi* (bread) and *aromatiko* (perfumed) will rekindle lineages. It is in the kitchens, landscapes, and myths that a particularly feminine sensibility is claimed in words, and names, that travel between languages and terrains as 'Greek women form//the most beautiful/mouths when speaking.'"

—Adrianne Kalfopoulou, author of *The re in Refuge*

Poetry Collections by Catherine Strisik

Goat, Goddess, Moon (Holy Cow! Press, 2025)
Insectum Gravitis (Main Street Rag, 2019)
The Mistress (3: A Taos Press, 2016)
Thousand-Cricket Song (Plain View Press, 2010,
second edition, 2016)

GOAT, GODDESS, MOON

Poems

Catherine Strisik

Holy Cow! Press
Duluth, Minnesota
2025

Kore, a gift to the goddess Athena, daughter of Zeus, 520-510 BC, Marble from Paros (Acr. 670), Acropolis Museum, Athens. Photo: Giorgos Vitsaropoulos, 2017.
Author photograph by Morgan Timms.
Book and cover design by Anton Khodakovsky.

Printed and bound in the United States.
First printing, Fall, 2025
10 9 8 7 6 5 4 3 2 1

Library of Congress Cataloging-in-Publication Data
Strisik, Catherine, author.
Goat, goddess, moon / poems by Catherine Strisik.
Other titles: Goat, goddess, moon (Compilation)
Duluth, Minnesota : Holy Cow! Press, 2025.
LCCN 2024053110 (print) | LCCN 2024053111 (ebook)
ISBN 9781666406979 (trade paperback) | ISBN 9781666406986 (kindle edition)
LCGFT: Poetry.
LCC PS3619.T7537 G63 2025 (print) | LCC PS3619.T7537 (ebook) |
DDC 811/.6--dc23/eng/20250116
LC record available at https://lccn.loc.gov/2024053110
LC ebook record available at https://lccn.loc.gov/2024053111

Holy Cow! Press projects are funded in part by grant awards from the Ben and Jeanne Overman Charitable Trust, the Elmer L. and Eleanor J. Andersen Foundation, the Lenfestey Family Foundation, the Woessner Freeman Family Foundation and by gifts from generous individual donors. We are grateful to Springboard for the Arts for their support as our fiscal sponsor.

Holy Cow! Press books are distributed to the trade by Consortium Book Sales & Distribution, c/o Ingram Publisher Services, Inc., 210 American Drive, Jackson, TN 38301.

For inquiries, please write to: *Holy Cow! Press,* Post Office Box 3170, Mount Royal Station, Duluth, MN 55803.
Visit *www.holycowpress.org*

For my mother

In memory of
Hariklea and Andreas Samaras
Georgia Samaras Kilonis

Acknowledgements

My appreciation to the following online and print publications where the following poems have been previously published or are forthcoming in sometimes earlier forms and with different titles:

Café Review: *"Kaliméra, Kaliméra"*
Comstock Review: "Pulp," "Agora"
Ergon: Greek/American Arts & Letters: "27 Romanou," "The Soup, *Magirítsa*," "From Trapezítsa"
Ginosko Literary Journal: "*Aikaterína,*" "Katerína, this poem is immortalizing," "Bone Cavity"
Lothlorien Poetry Journal: "With Panagía"
Mediterranean Poetry: "*Kalispera,*" "The Sea," "Diaphanous," "Ceremony: A Kind of Greek Woman," "Quake"
Pen Norway: "Grevená People"
Silk Road Review: "Braid"
Soundings East: "Fried Eggplant Sandwiches"
SWWIM: "In My Grandfather's Living Room"
The Maynard: "Humid Weather," "Me of Me"
Unbroken Journal: "vein," "Centuries Old Kako Mati"
Zócalo Public Square: "I Wake In Heraklion With Lady Beetles"

In Gratitude

My heartfelt gratitude to my publisher, Jim Perlman of Holy Cow! Press who showed enthusiasm, care, and dedication to this body of work from the moment an excerpt was presented to him.

My profound love to my grandfather, Andreas Samaras who in a thick journal wrote of his childhood and diaspora, his love of his homeland and his love of America. Much appreciation to the Acropolis Museum and Ministry of Greek Culture for granting permission to use Kore 670 displayed at the Acropolis Museum in Athens for the book cover. My warmest thanks to the poets who generously offered their comments for the book: Lauren Camp, Veronica Golos, Adrianne Kalfopoulou, George Kalogeris, and Mervyn Taylor.

My thanks into eternity for their profound critiques, and inspiration over many years on one or two poems or the entirety of the collection: Scott Cairns, Thomas Centolella, Lise Goett, Veronica Golos, Alexander Long, Sawnie Morris, Jean Nordhaus, Kate O'Neil, Joan Ryan, Jamie Ross, Judith Thompson, and Leslie Ullman.

To George Kalogeris, my deepest appreciation for his vision and guidance, his harmony in our shared culture, and for suggesting *Goat, Goddess, Moon* as the collection's title.

Thank you to the Lakkos Artist Residency in Heraklion, Crete from where many early drafts of these poems were written in 2016, and to Sara Kafatou who generously offered to me her home in Fortetsa, Heraklion in 2023 in which to write and from where the manuscript neared completion.

And, always my gratitude and love to Dimitra Eleni, light of my life.

Contents

I. My Villages: Amygdaliés; Trapezítsa 1
Seed 3
Kaliméra, Kaliméra 6
vein 7
Genealogy 8
For Sacred Purposes: The Boy, the Herd, the Gold 9
Koύkla 10
Filigree 11
Braid 12
Grevená People 13
The Soup, *Magirítsa* 14
In My Grandfather's Living Room 16
Fried Eggplant Sandwiches 18
From Trapezítsa 19
With Panagía 20
Haríklea 21
Centuries Old Kako Mati 22

II. My Labyrinth: Heraklion 23
Upon Seeing a Used Condom on the Ground 24
27 Romanou 25
Labyrinth 27
Cretan Olive Oil 31
kalispera 32
I Wake in Heraklion with Lady Beetles 33
Taverna Zaxaris at Paleokastro Beach 35
The Sea 37
Diaphanous 38
Goddess to Goddess 39
Agora 40
After Playing Für Elise 42

Pulp 43
Goat, Goddess, Moon 45
Dawning 46
The Dog and Me About a Month Later 47
Quake 48
Sefer 49

III. My Name: *Katerína* 51
Humid Weather 52
In Reality, Menopause 54
Aikaterína 55
Katerína, this poem is immortalizing 64
In the Home of Agile Light 65
White Orchid 66
Ceremony: A Kind of Greek Woman 69
Bone Cavity 71
Me of Me 72

Notes 73
About the Author 77

And I said

I shall burn the
fat thigh-bones of
a white she-goat
on her altar
—Sappho

There is beauty in our roots.
—Luis Alberto Urrea

Ψ

My Villages: Amygdaliés; Trapezítsa

Seed

I love this story—
My great grandmother was my great grandmother in Amygdaliés.
My grandmother always knelt in the chamomile with her.
They loved the small golden flowers in the field—
This is not a story,
more the truth and a memory,
a eulogy of sorts by the time I arrived
something replenished when up to my knees
here in oregano and lemon balm
now a hint of chamomile.

My great grandmother. My great grandmother in Amygdaliés.
My grandmother always knelt in the chamomile with her.
This is not a story,
more the truth.
They pressed deep into the forgiving soil
a walnut seed in the far corner of their land.
Then left in 1916 in February on the SS Vasilef Constantinos
for America.

If I say walnut and seed I mean
great grandmother and grandmother
now an eighty-foot walnut tree
in June. It's my birthday.
They embroidered onto their hems
their home's flowers, buried in the earth,
buried with their hands also, some gold,
shaped as a bracelet and two rings;

My great grandmother was my great grandmother. In Amygdaliés.

My grandmother always knelt in the chamomile with her.
If I dig with their intent, ecstatic beneath this tree, stopping
only to breathe their breath as a calm catches
the encrusted, pale yellow of them—

then please consider this:

here is the love
poem with the seed,
the source of what was
buried and what was dug
what is nutrient
protein, starch, their oils now
held by the walnut's bark.
I prepare

not only my lips with balm but my spot on my earth:
which I already know
its embryo
the interior greenery of us:

My great grandmother died at 42 with a swollen belly.
My grandmother died in a hospital of heart failure at 94.
They will always be
heartwood, and so I lean into

the bark now and the stillness.
The walnut bark, it reduces aching in the heart.
In the story,

later in the day there is rain.
They exhale once
more. I inhale.
We pause,
of the earth,

briefly.

Kaliméra, Kaliméra

Clean white satin, white
cake, tenderly-torn whisper
this gift is for you.

Pearled barley, village
honey, pistachios, and
walnuts, the spoon raised

to lips. The sound—the sound
begins to pronounce—
Katerína. Once.

vein

if he left by foot ( ) or donkey ( ) or cart and donkey ( ) or cart and horse from his hometown in 1913 the second Balkan War having started in June in central Macedonia ( ) did he carry in his pocket soil from Trapezítsa did he carry in his bag slung over his shoulder or in his other pocket or wrapped in fabric cut from his mother's hem *paximathia* so that he'd have wheat and olive oil for the journey ( ) at 16 years old ( ) this being the last time he'd see his mother and he was a handsome sweet son and I know because he was a handsome sweet grandfather and ( ) how did his mother know of America from the village of 65 people ( ) how did she tell her second son to save his life he must go during the raisin and drought crisis during fragmentation of a culture and arrive at 17 to the rest of his life ( ) maybe because he held my hand the way his mother held his with affectionate fondling as though reaching through the dermis to the fascia the muscle to the vein where I am the rest of his story.

Genealogy

Throughout the summer
        on Baltimore Street, the scent of basil
and dill. I could inhale

those verdant herbs from his pen,
        the scratch scratch scratch across his ledger's roughened
yellowed pages. And yes, his hand carved the letters

though with a hammer, chisel, and stone.
        Always his pipe, filled with tobacco.
Write, *Katerína,* about the basil, my grandfather tells me.

For Sacred Purposes: The Boy, the Herd, the Gold

Not very far away from Trapezítsa the land is layered
with foundations from before and before
and before. On the mountain the boy
holds a goat in his hands.
See the mountain rise in his face
and there raised in glorification, the goat
offered in sacrifice.

*

Grandfather wrote as a boy he picked up some fingers
broken from a golden hand embedded
in a ditch not far from his hometown, noticed
the wall, 15 feet high, *khrysos*
halfway up from the banking when pulled,
six hands beautiful
women's hands.

*

The hands looked natural
he wrote. They had veins, hair,
the fingernails painted many colors
he wrote, women's beautiful
hands grasping one another on the day
his grandfather sent him to watch part
of the herd.

Koúkla

For you I call a fresh pear
sweet, innocent with wanderings,
chin, cleft from, a great great archeological find.

Filigree

My grandfather told me *I pried the hands*
of gold from the wall, all six of them,
beautiful, then I burned all but
one in the fire to melt gold My daughter
loves women's hands and I watch her
hands because there is a precision
in her finger-play since birth, their
shape, splendid I see, yes,
splendid, our shapes.

Braid

In a Greek kitchen everything turns translucent:

—tissue paper, colored syrup,
green bowls, even sesame seeds.

In my grandmother's, I open when alone
the many-bundled *psomi*. I break
off a chunk, its circular shape, buttery on my lips.

One street over from *Saint Katerina*, there is a Greek bakery, *Elpis*:

Yeast bubbles, dough coils into braids. Sun's warmth
at the counter where I stand eye level
to the scented breads, inhale inhale

inhale our three thousand years'
rising.

Grevená People

We take our places at the stove casually
flaunting our flaws, our fractured English
and our wooden-handled spoons and give
the appearance of the attentive, square and
straight-backed. We gather to stir lamb shank
stew. Within the stir, a hand gesture's resemblance,
our language prepared with the moisture and *baa*
of the mother lamb. When I ask for a taste, speak
quickly about the ingredients, you each hold
a spoon to my mouth. The ingredients taste
of wool and shepherds. I taste our
resemblance, our sacrifice. We have fallen
in love because it is June, and raining
hard. For a moment, we gaze
toward the flock on the hillside.

The Soup, Magirítsa

I taste their entrails
and organs their
sacrifice at midnight

our tongue

as the lamb and goats
of Grevená bleat around us

udders pinkened
released lips

hollowed where the consecrated contused
or faith, maybe

the butchered, scented with frankincense, and
myrrh and basil breeze
so silent
in moon spots, in my mother's kitchen, the egg, and olive oil

our Greek
profile, her heart, liver, her lungs I yearn
to squeeze
even now, the lemon.

The well-looked-into eyes.
The dill chopped, and leaves of romaine.

The exhalation   *adore me,*   the livid

communion

on breath, the wine itself. My mother
cleans throats expectant
as birth, metered.

In My Grandfather's Living Room

Say it. Say. While standing
on your head: the Greek alphabet,
and I will toss you pennies. Keep going.

It's an alphabet. It's the first alphabet.
It's the alphabet said by Alexander the Greek.
Say it. Alexander the Greek. *Say Alexander the*

Great. History says we are related by DNA.
No, but we really are. We are.
See my crooked teeth. Twenty-four

letters, chant as though we always existed: Antiquity, Ovum,
Alpha Beta Gamma
that's three pennies for you.

An alphabet that cries, waves, swoons
in the air at Delphi circling the stadium,
everybody's running the length.

We sing in the alphabet where it becomes sumptuous,
and the alphabet is melodic when striking ancient.
Crescent. A blue root. Over here, a copper cup

with water for drinking and water for bathing
the inside of your mouth
when you speak fluently. Hear, my voice-

silhouetted-dedicated-life force
a warmed shape resembling Omega.

Round your lips. O-me-ga

Early mornings, it's the smallest birds that perch
around the feeders, pick seed. And song.
Epsilon, Iota.

A full mouth. Yes.
The crown of your head lights up the room,
and now scattered pennies.

Fried Eggplant Sandwiches

No one speaks English. No one
speaks softly. All the sounds — chewing
of eggplant, swallowing of eggplant,
and digesting of eggplant —
are in Greek. No doubt
defecation of eggplant, purple-robed,
round-thighed, and thick-hipped will be
in Greek. No telling the difference
between one Greek and another.
As if each descends from Alexander,
like Pappoú always says.
In Thia Bargas' kitchen
we eat fried eggplant sandwiches.
I believe him.

From Trapezítsa

Again, this morning, we gather, with dried tobacco leaves
crumbled inside pockets. Uncle Lampos, a small man, carries
American cash.
Erató, his blond niece, pulls a beauty salon chair, curlers, and a hair

dryer all with her strong back. My grandfather, laughing, slouches
with the weight of his garden slung over his shoulder. The old
butcher, his most tasty cut. These mornings

they sit in dim light as I boil my egg.
A big stainless pot, reflection from every angle.
Grandfather, in love with the green vegetables, sings of the garden.

The butcher's scarred hands play cat's cradle. Uncle Lampos
embraces his American cash. Erató practices her English.
The yolk hardens. I wear my bathrobe open.

With Panagía

We say Greek. We say church. We say Greek Church. We say Greek School. We say Sunday School. We say the Father Son and Holy Spirit. We say Byzantine cross, 18 K. We say Baltimore Street. We say Haverhill, Massachusetts. We say Yiayía and Pappoυs. We say Greek village. Amygdaliés. Trapezitsa. We say immigrant. We say Hellenic. We say Thalassémia. We say Greek dance in Boston. We say Greek Community Center. Ahépa. We say Greek boys. We say our grandmothers say, "Marry a Greek boy." We say féta, psomí, katsiróla, fenékia, dolmάthes, stóma, thía, thío. We say our grandmothers say, "What, not marrying a Greek boy?" We say probably not. We say ouch. Our faces. We say crocheted potholders. We say knitted slippers. We say embroidered tablecloths. We say kouzíni, foύrnos, and mousakάs. We say Greek dogmas. Do not cross your legs in church. We say matriarchal. Spanikópeta. We say shrill and fast language. We say broken Greek. I speak broken Greek. We say fluent Greek. We say Greek gypsy, Greek Turk, Communist Greek, Island Greek, Greek mother, city Greek, village Greek. We say Greek Easter. We say grapevine. We say sacrifice. We say lamb. We say roasted lamb head on our best china. We say Greek friendship, rooted (at first we were four). We say when we go to Greece together. We say our grandmothers say, "Well, he'd better be a doctor then." (and so, he was). We say prάsa. We say chórta. The young ones because they are tender. We say mothers who dance on tables. (and so, I did). They say teach your daughters right. (as I do). We know. They say water the tulips at our graves in the Greek section. (I promised, and as I do). We sigh (because we are always so close to home), in Greek.

Haríklea

This is a private moment

where I unzip
the plastic bag and sometimes remove her

apron hold it

in my hands press
into it my nose

and open mouth

sucking in
sucking in

her scent butter and beaten
eggs and sugar.

Centuries Old Kako Mati

The old gypsy chooses me – stands three inches from my face inside the Thessaloniki Bus Terminal where I drink bottled water eyes my turquoise beads – eyes me right into my eyes and then eyes my skirt with its many colors – speaks *not nice* I hear the tone *not nice* too close in a dialect I've never heard yet recognize from stories I'd been told – perhaps her limp the ankle-length skirt and the hem frayed though there are no sheep no hillsides steep and rocky no not here at the terminal no not here where there are no rays today in any direction leading out of this city – no dismembering of the sacrificial animals the goat the lamb certainly there are no cherries in late April – a tone *not nice not nice* too fast for me not by any means beautiful but my feet touch the sea – because something she's said – with her eyes faded indigo in a gypsy Greek tongue that's strange to my ear – and now the pain in my gut horizontal and I dazed by her malicious gaze and where is the toilet as though her hands sun-toughened pull out of me a cry and cramping – what her spell wants for me as her voice pickaxes the morning light – to scathe not my innocence after all I am on the edge of a greater age – is to throw off my poise her eye steady and practiced and because of the sudden pull – because I've forgotten astonished by her curses – to hold up my hands between us as a shield to spit spit spit into my armpit where is my crucifix where is my beaded eye oh mother oh god my grandmother nowhere to be found to wash my body with mud to break the viscosity – without protection my flora unmistakably altered.

Ψ

My Labyrinth: Heraklion

Upon Seeing a Used Condom on the Ground

Not that I want to know who
ejaculated in the night on Navarinou, whose cylindrical
chute came close to my parked rental car, who
clutched somebody below or above or beside, who
moaned in off-verse during an unfamiliar lyric poem's
recital, who named the night Lethe, maybe
Aphrodite, maybe, the condom that protected
where the deep of the river flows, the high-pitched
screams of cats from every curve on this precipice, damn it
god, let me tell you about my, own, salvation.

27 Romanou

In puce fitting curves of my then slendered-
by-grief body

you served me goat stew at the square
wooden table covered by a red tablecloth

the evening my heels and my suitcase's wheels muddied
from an earlier rain in Heraklion where I walked the labyrinth

for hours. I felt faint the humidity and my erratic woman's cycles
in proximity to the goat

parts in my bowl with cracked wheat that had soaked and dry-roasted
for months in the sun.

I wanted to be stroked
moist with the Cretan Sea.

There was a candelabra
and a delicate revolution

in my mind between the want and the need.
Hungry like the line of tiny ants

that entered in and out of the decaying hole in the wall of the kitchen
though I had been mistaken before with the thought of being desired.

You served me goat stew—
what I'd never before eaten.

It tasted good.

Later we walked through darkened rooms dated from the Ottoman Empire to the steep staircase to a room with a single bed and a light

weight blanket. All night I listened to the rumbling and hissing of cats, their many torn voices.

Labyrinth

1

All along, it's been here:
curves, the barks of dogs —

        grey sky and warning;
so many widows in black

        in cobblestoned alleyways,
this way back, this curve. To Fortetsa.

Now there is just
        a scream, my own

blood soaked / through my / pant leg / a golden
scruff of a dog / split me

and I must make peace with this.

2

        When I first cut
the lavender roses —

        open petaled, gay, and fragranced
close to nostalgia —

        having taken a wrong turn, my always poor
sense of direction —

    though this time I could hear / church bells close
and me dressed for the evening in new

    pink sneakers, a little laughter,
a little hello, and wanting the bath

later just to do this:
                    ahhhhhhh

Will drinking licorice tea — soothe —
and which alley is to home?

3

Each time I wake
the dog's ripped apart
my calf.

On my walk towards Knossos where
fenced geese, ducks, and chickens waddled,

a startled dog, an unkempt offspring,
offspring of pre-history fanged
and fury, the caretaker within a pained
olive groves' memory.

Misunderstanding.

Springtime.
    And me.

Difficult to carry
the burden of fallen cultures, and be the deliverer
of shear madness.
At me.
        While I'm out simply for an evening walk.

Somewhere there is a farmer who has poured
        water into the feeding bins, so that this dog, ancestral, will remain:
alive, and this/our chance encounter.

4

The cobblestones are just outside the rose pathway, and metal gates,
        and if I walk again

I will see as far as the sea.

The cobblestone alleyways house the dogs,
        their spines' broken curves, a sliver of light, a garden
                                        of fennel,

and soon-to be-ripe
        apricots.

        Today the sky warns,
the elderly woman again bent

        over with a paint brush
repainting her white wall.

The piano waits for me. In one month
I've taught myself to play Beethoven's Für Elise, touch

lightly the keys. Weightless, the church bells the rising
bark of a dog.

A scent of me hangs still in their air.

Cretan Olive Oil

She suggests this corner of Fortetsa
protects the soul with an abundance
of koroneiki olives.

Their flavor – *aromatiko'*–

Some bruising of my tongue,
and smoke.

kalispera

In the dusk around the corner by the butcher shop
a few white-haired men look up from their circled chairs,

cigarettes, pipes, their leather shoes, clean
and shiny where I muse

every time I round the corner to this
opening at the end of this long alleyway, the stillness, the white-

capped sea, the spring blossoms, where they listen
in the *pure and familiar silence*

that is home.
When I stop what I'm doing, what appears like nothing really, a walk,

and listen, their *kalispera*
my *kalispera* in unison *kalispera*.

It's my precise pronunciation, my eyes
invisible behind brown-tinted sunglasses, my always quick

amble, my impossible tranquility
in the dusk's darkening the alto barks of wandering startled dogs,

their aloneness, my aloneness, every time I'm aware of the fricatives
of the Cretan language and the olives

on their shared table, soaked in brine.

I Wake in Heraklion with Lady Beetles

I am soft with healing after
I am luxuriant with good fortune after
I am cloaked by lady beetles a scent of salted olive, my nature after
all means spacious means rhododendron and a pretty mouth.

If I give the impression of canopied with black spots after
my sorrow believe me when I say I am in pursuit of myself and a kiss and
might after I be a ridge on Mount Ida might local winegrowers and cicadas
might my hollow after deep between my thighs be my greeting braced —

There's femininity a softening
I'd cherish the softening
I'd forgotten.

I'd cherish the softening
Holy is the body

its roundness the flesh
its brine a sweet

secret a shuttered
body a *cherished* resumé.

There's so much song even in heartache and my heart the female
body after bird melody my simple request after

the seeded bread I'd bought at the base of Lasíthi flavored
with orange rind. I am a Greek woman's body
I was told in the marketplace after buying a potato and sea bream

the morning planes flew overhead celebrating Saint Minas when two vendors said *you are one of us* The earthy.

Polite. Greek.
Fluid.

And the lady beetles they mean I am composed of a million single cries.

Taverna Zaxaris at Paleokastro Beach

One cat, not yet oblivious
to his needs, yet oblivious

to his condition, staggers
to my table at the taverna, begging

for food from a mouth wrecked
and crooked, mindless as he tries

to sing. A couple from another table look,
then get up and walk away. The fur

around his mouth filthy, with dirt
and derangement. I don't know

what to do. One eye clutches
me. The right eye

I notice when I look long
enough, is missing, so there

is a hole there.
I peel grilled shrimp

with my fingers. Other cats,
young, vocalize close by.

Some weep. Some chatter.
A child from another table

stands up to see. The waiter
says *fy'-ge* to the cats and they

scatter except for the one.
Who hums

from the beach? The cliffs
here wrap and loom.

Teeth clench. I want to know who
prays, who weeps, who shovels

the sediment when his body
is no fur, is no bone. When his voice

is silent.

The Sea

I arrived early to the sea, voices
of women in the cove, some
topless in the Cretan Sea, bobbing, and I,
swimming out
from the shore where others lay
on flat rocks, smoking, laughing, draped in seaweed,
their local Greek dialect cured like the body after
swimming. I held my breasts,
under the eyes of Thalassa, half-submerged,

she who still spawns, salted, calming,
inhuman the body rises
in the light the moon
sends back.

Diaphanous

Tempered by daybreak my sometimes,
suckled from four directions,
spirit, enjoying particularly in October

my hands, their curvature, along the path of Lasíthi,
and there are almonds, and delicate
orange slices, too, and in the distance

the familiar bark of a dog, how
in Kastamonítsa we are caught
in newness and disobedience of mid-autumn when

even the plants and Sea have little order where
in this brief undulate I get away

with the g in goddess.

Goddess to Goddess

-upon seeing a girl dancing on the edge of Fortetsa

We mean moist path as myth don't we?
Moist meaning *opa* after *opa*

Are you the *opa* and am I the dance?
Touching bare-

footed wild-weeded fennel
or *agape*

Maybe *agape* is what we mean
agape on the edge of Fortetsa to bend

Yes bend closer
mythed/unmythed to *Kríti*.

Agora

I love what I love. The man at the fish market
yesterday coming from behind
the counter to show me, guts torn out with his fingers right in front of me.

When I told him I wanted six smelt only,
he asked if I was in Heraklion alone.
I said friends, I am here with friends, I said

to stop his flirtation, the smelt maybe dangerous, the bones soft.
He knew I was lying.
He pointed to my olive blouse with lilac flowers, low-

draped front, maybe pull it up a little he said. I love
what I love. The woman, after handing her two onions
and one garlic bulb gave me the price in Greek.

oh, I thought you were one of us, your look

My Monday dress mauve and fitted, sports socks inside clogs, sweater
draped and hooded, and no eye make-up.

you look like one of us

When I return again to the man
to buy fish, cod fillets are beautifully cleaned and displayed
on ice. His hands

glisten. I love what I love.

If I spend one year here I will again speak Greek fluently he says,
the hungry part of me revealed,

knowing when I eat what must be good   I *must chew*
gently.

After Playing Für Elise

When the temptation rises
and the fountain, its
Arabic inscription faded,
remembers to flow, at midnight,
its waters, I stand in the spring
winds of Fortetsa squeezing
oranges.

Pulp

Tell me the moment of shuddering in Crete

The one when my skin moistened from the sea?
The one with drilling grinding cleaving workmen's
voices across the alley my hands
when I awaken boundless on my flesh? Forgiving.

Forgiven.

In the night I strip off my nightgown one loud crash
on the roof, cats grumble and growl.

My upper arms having lost firmness, and my
lowered lids.

The grey-striped cat that balances above on the wall watching
me, the cat with an ear torn and matted fur

the cat who's been beaten who perhaps
on the patio outside my bedroom, vomits,
not sensing my need for lavender
and improvisation

in a small space.   My need to sway I mean

swoon. My nipples, or the peculiar
mouth
for love's sake
is so often in command like the alphabet

in any language, the black salted olives from the commoner's
market decided on only
after tasting five varieties.

Now, tell me the moment of shuddering in Crete

He has warm hands. Thick, too.
The lifeline long and deep like the Samaria Gorge.
I do not know what day of the week it is while lost
in Heraklion's labyrinth, my inner thighs, pulp, back
of neck heat with the thought of him. Three weeks

of scraping sawing sanding workmen's
song loud and second-hand smoke.

That this straw-seated chair and I have become more
than mere acquaintances
here with the trail of ants. As though textured

with an inspired drainage.

Last night by 1 a.m. I passed out with the consumption of too much
wine and raki. Well let me say we do not even know each other.

Yes?

My vision blurred at Knossos.

My arms opened there

was an eagle. My throat, in prayer, wide.

Goat, Goddess, Moon

So aroused I'd become by the goat-tending
myth I could see the grainy grasses on her
tongue at the food bin, and heard

the suckling nymph Aretusa
as she said *pomegranate*
and *prickly pear*. Greek women form

the most beautiful
mouths when speaking, and she pronounced
Knossos like this

K-NO-SSOS

her voice, again, translucent—
as goddess-like October—and now my breath
smells like sweetgrass

burning in the evening. In Crete,
carob bows low from branches. I didn't
know carob, crescent-shaped, grew on trees.

Aretusa said *carob* & *Crete*. I was kissed
by a goat last night on my right hand the wire
fence sharp
                    the three-quarter
                                        moon a bright lantern.

Dawning

It was four in the morning
or maybe four thirty

not quite light, the bed
far away from the window, pillows propped:
predawn—completely quiet—except for the cats' yowls.
A solar light, I knew, shaped a small circle.
The Greek music's hum earlier, from someone's car radio, gone.

No one could see the cats. But,
they were already at a high pitch
had *become incapable of caution*

Their mouths open wide—a bird between them
one wing flapping still

when I got out of bed to see,
their shapes in the light circle.
The ceiling fan spun above my head.

Pleasure of bird figure between
those crouching cats, ears flattened;
rapid chattering, backs arched—after all
the sky now pinkened.

The Dog and Me About a Month Later

I write on inheritance. I probably
closed my eyes.
It is the north

coast of Crete the contour
of the cracked road named Navarinou
falling towards the sea falling

into rooftops below, a dog's den, a field of wild
ones; oregano and fennel.
I write on inheritance, a broom handle sliding

across space the 11 pm earthquake.
In it, the slide is neither my shortness of breath nor
blood flow nor a collision of two

breaths; in it is our disobedient and good selves.
Does falling toward the sea even matter?
An olive grove stands equally powerful, this month later,

dry on the soulful slope, lastly there is sweat in the air.
There is the one dog who, at high pitch, barks, "I'm afraid, how
is the nightmare wound on your calf?"

I'm, afraid, too, now, of all dogs: the purist, strangest, poetic
dog in the whitewashed alley; and because there are now vertical
lines above my upper lip: the inheritance shaped like my whole body

curved, I murmur,
everyday my fingers caress and re-settle into your wound.

Quake

Petals sway in unison
with the boom that raises
the sea, all females

sing static. I pull back
my thinning hair with hairpins —
                                        in case the quakes' aftermath —
and take pleasure in the moans

of my own Greek ache. After-affects a little
coarse like a salt scrub. It feels risky
to not look below and not look

                                        above everything
extraordinary and bright bright blue.

Sefer

I love the blue, the unrestrained, the white
mountainside villages cobble-
stoned and the calm

voice of the workman with the most
handsome face I've ever seen peering through
a glassless window my scraping

car against his pickup in the too-tight alley
his simple words
    left right   left right   left right

directing me out of tightness I love
not him specifically but him because he looks
and knows I feel a fool in Archanes. My feet

naked. The basil in windows.
I'm swollen-with-May orbs
in this myth. When I love I love

the plum wine. O Heraklion,
this is about
myself. Adrift.

Ψ

My Name: *Katerína*

Humid Weather

When you search, you will find me

well-mannered with the linen handkerchief,
the one I used to get away

with dabbing. I strolled, in Crete, sweating
in the *agora* with iced fish

and Greek men, some of whom leaned
to touch me. Church bells rang. I did not count how many.

I chose you, the distant
foreigner because you

wrote tongue-tied and slept tied
to me and remedied me

to the flushed body, and then
to terra cotta. In humid weather I am

raw to the primal.
No white beans, no straw, no woman's cycles, only

the Ottoman house,
the crazy owner's singing rising

inside the high walls missing stones
of phyllite in the decrepit alley in the neighborhood of Lakkos.

This week the humidity in the *agora* is so thick
no one sees me as real, and I see no one else as real, either.

In one of my books, you will read about me
as a paramour on the flat rooftop

in my fragrant garden, in tiger
lily chiffon, the crook of my elbow

bared, and my hymns,
the evening star—nothing hidden, I

sightsee for pleasure.
Curious, do you? Are you warmed by wind

at the very moment I am warmed by the wind?
Curious, are you damp, somewhere, in haze?

In Reality, Menopause

I say   I will
kiss your face until the mark
enflamed
is my mouth

in reality

Crete is the island of
          remnants

in reality

All I want is —
          say my name

I am not   a beggar
          in my sweated sheets

I say
          nothing

my buckling   knees
          dry mouth   dry eyes

eye gnats   suck   dry my tears
          nausea   I need

air and   my left   ear its particular
          heat here on —

Aikaterína

Ψ

Katerína is my Greek name and I say it only at church when receiving communion or I write it now just to see the Greek κατερίνα though I wasn't born in Greece and though my name day falls on November 25 Saint Katherine eloquent martyr and though there was no way walking alone the Venetikos the sound from Pan who leaned against a wall roughing my attention away from the old stone bridge my thoughts of Portitsa Gorge and the otters denned in empty hollows no he didn't know my name but he ruffled my attention, as if he'd called out *Katerína* as if he'd annunciated each sound

/k/a/t/er/i/n/a

as if he'd tongued my silk, dawn's unfamiliar birdsong, church bells, even my blistered toes, cobblestones, the market's gold coffee, bouquets of peach tulips, and the young man with angel blue eyes who sliced unfamiliar for me to sample, cheese, hard and salty, the saleswoman my age her kiss on my cheeks the second time I returned noticing her short fingernails and worn flats. She handed me velvet sapphire heels to match my new dress, she said; sometimes the sound of my name in Greek is the Christmas cactus in my dining room that blooms three times a year, that's how infrequently I hear *Katerína* said aloud, and sometimes when aloud it's a twist of the village wrist or Thía Georgia my godmother the sacred spray from the Cretan Sea or a typical Greek day which for no one else but me means love. So my attention toward because its sound

/k/a/t/er/i/n/a

Katerina Katerina Katerina

is love.

Ψ

The Venetikos with its gentle
rush. An exclamation or grunt
or a moan. His face (maybe) handsome
(maybe) crude. His hands (maybe) rapid
my attention dropping his face
his hands his hooves shaking his

half seduction out of the sound
of my, my rough Greek my Greek name
is my Greek confoundedness that
croons my half-resilient throat white
murmur by the river my, echo

echo echo Greek name *Katerina,*
my Greek name is Never on Sunday,
my Greek name is Sultana,
Hariklea, my Greek name is
walnut tree, gardener, my Greek

name is crochet, Zorba, my Greek
name is please   bittersweet me;
but sometimes the unexpected
occurs and the Greek

Katerina

hides in a vessel in Knossos
or in a fissure in olive
green stone falling into the
Aegean, my blue silk dress
does not show enough shadow,

enough of the body's silhouette
I have little use for the heartbeat
of the world, eloquent martyr,
as I stand opening my goddess
dress on cliffs.

Ψ

My name is *Katerina* though
I look wholesome in scoop-necked pink
chiffons, did I mention the blue
dress bought in Thessaloniki
has bell-shaped sleeves that catch the wind
like angel wings, that when I dine

at my hand-crafted walnut table
I confess I've never made love
on though it is as wide and long
as a full-size bed designed by
many imaginations I
am bordered on the east by barbed

wire the white horse sensing alfalfa
on my side sweeter, fresher; on
the south hooves in the middle
of nights in spring; in autumn

the bear and her cubs' predawn call
out to one another the spring-

fed pond nearly dry. Am I trusted
by all? No, not all I was told
to my face. Until then I thought
I was adored by all.   I cut
my hair an ancient ceremony.
My lover wears his halfway

down his back sometimes loosens when
we make love then I see my lover
is corn husk and December embers
in the throes of unresisted heat
my heart both delivers, and aches.

Ψ

Katerina is my Greek name
murmured and body plentiful
aroused red below bath water's
rendition rhythmically
controlled by a finger placed on
my woman's hope.

Ψ

Skull still shock-hard oh
cloudless night the helm
of the body *That*
story again Pan's
recognizable

song and urgency
swinging from Grevená
to Thessaloniki.
My recognizable
rough sound.

Ψ

Where is the white horse
wandering spring loose
to the fence line?

Ψ

Yes, my name is *Katerina.*
The earliest birdsong, 4 am.
Most from cottonwoods, thin branches,
surrounding ponds. The creek flows
east to west. Far from Grevená.

Far from the Venetikos.
Far from Pan's concrete century's
beckoning the creases and knobs
my skull numbed by gravitation
of late March three days before

Easter. I'm
shiver.

The horse pisses in the desolate
field the teepee wrecked by spring winds
no apple trees in Jenny's orchard

this view from my cabin window
failing while the weight of white

butterflies fluttering low
to the earth I have not softened
my belly long enough the bed
fluffed yet cold. For surely my
lover, if he knew I was

crying. If I do not remove
the dead soon these vulnerable
branches soon their impact in
fatigued
fall.

Ψ

My village Trapezitsa. My Greek name is the name
of the village aunts is the name of my grandfather's
mother is the name of the tobacco leaves is gesture's circular
twist of the wrist recorded in DNA in each sunrise and leaf
intelligence I looked

Ψ

to the sound along
the Venetikos,
Pan's face his hands that
wandered the river's
edge and all passersby
I'm still crying nine
months after having
my ovaries removed

Ψ

and know it is good to cry with my face covered

Ψ

the tulips blossom from my
cabin's south-facing window

Ψ

under blankets, and skinned I've felt endangered
eros rub.

Ψ

He dresses me slipping my legs
back into panties, my feet into

sandals, with the delicacy
of dressing the adored dead,
the kisses there afterward and
there the continued swell who

ever imagined the body
at 60 would continue with spring

run-off, with all the sense of
dirt.

Ψ

Tonight a fox, rust darted
across the highway and as I,
about to hit it, hit my break,
it stopping momentarily,
turned to me, then disappeared
into darkness. Did I say yet
that Jesus laid supine on

the floor next to my childhood
bed at Yiάyia's and Pappoύ's,
I enlightened when all else
dark that yes, he wore white robes and
yes, I saw his face. I saw
Jesus while a child, and he spoke

Katerina Katerina Katerina Katerina Katerina

Ψ

Say it. Again.

Ψ

In the ikonostási
Panagia, the red egg, the
holy water, the oil, did I
say I may have been sacrificed
to birth my daughter and her
daughter and her daughter.

Ψ

In my mouth he places syrup from his
mouth, velvet from, my god,
no wonder he drinks me like he
does the fluid of birth of dawn
my fluid my lips into my throat my
life my god my gold my hold my
love, this profiled urge. Remember
me. Spring's menagerie.

Ψ

κατερίνα

Ψ

Have I written that I carry
rocks with me from one life to
another? And my oils flow from
my fingers when cut from my hands?

Ψ

Three mallards fly through cottonwoods their wings the sound
a crack.

Katerína, this poem is immortalizing

the cat also, who—after your plea
to stop his lurch at others in the middle

of too many nights, and for what, a scent
of yellow rose, the coolness beneath a lemon tree,

the halting blood-packed earth of Fortetsa
something, so certain his inscrutable stare back at you last night—

is not curled up on your last morning
close to the almond tree, and you do not hear

the feverish barks of dogs either
and like these angry, generation-old dogs,

you too have slept on your back
in distress, to avoid, being too close

to an unfamiliar surface, a pillow not smelling
right, or the earth, or a drip that might as well be a gushing river,

a sliver of light, and here you have heard your own heavy
breathing. Look at these vacant vagrant dogs and cats.

They have caught up with you. As prayer.
Or mist. Or breath.

In the Home of Agile Light

Even now,
weeks later,
I bandage my gash with gauze—

Not because there's blood,
nor pain,
nor the dog's vicious, emergent maul,

but to rehearse
mortality
to make the untender tender.

White Orchid

What is it about the lava rock. Or,
the sage grass always shaking out the wind
but tenderly, how soon.

*

The finikia I baked
          to ease, did taste like honey—

at 10:30 pm
          at my kitchen counter, after, the sweet butter

grated into, thickened, when down
          my shirt formed

moisture, a moment
I needed to taste.

*

          I am left-handed all my life

the world has revolved round.

*

Tawny eagle rising

how many beats to reach this
wingspan

this gesture?
Has he seen

me as risk, knowing
the woman

and the white orchid.

*

In certain southwestern light I am all the faces of my past.

*

Have you any idea the empathy of a neck?
It's a simple wind.

*

I've been allowed to cry
at many bedsides.
Oh.

Naked, too,
what winter is—

Cedar echoes the body echoes
the body.

*

In certain Aegean light I am all the faces of my past I hum

*

or —   no longer

draw in my knees to chest, and jaw
            like any other woman

            attempting hard

            not to tighten.

Ceremony: A Kind of Greek Woman

Water is served with coffee.
There's coffee for me
at Xanthi Hair Lounge
ordered for me from the coffee

and pastry shop next door.
While a new color saturates
my hair. There's bottled water
placed so gently before me as though

it were in a crystal glass I feel
I will cry. The gestures of the females here
careful, deliberate, like the tilt
of a head, and the mouths

that speak with fullness, tasting
the English language tender
in their mouths as the sounds
savored, are strewn together, so unbearably

sexy as though the lips and tongue
are full of want or romance or with
beating wings as if filled
with blessings that cannot be

contained, and outlined with
shades a bit darker than a lip color.
There's coffee, and sometimes a glass of water
on the tray, with sugar, and hazelnuts

and sultanas. Some are shaped like
the lower half of a Greek
woman, the waist, hips, buttocks,
the thighs this full shape impossibly

important. One dressed in black with a Byzantine
crucifix said this. Carry yourself as a Greek woman.
The water flows from springs in the highest mountains.
When drinking Dictamnus tea acknowledge

beauty in the nod of a head, the flair of a hand as
when a belly dancer swirls
her hands in the air. Her mouth, too full to be delicate.
Sometimes with the coffee there are two sugars.

Bone Cavity

My unpredictable want in its pose of yes
yes, my between teeth always taste sweet.

Here, village air scented with my blood scented with my
shawl and what's a scar?

My home promises fetish and icon, each night
from the old country, the 80-year-old blanket, skin bared,

scratched, some poem on my bed
lined with oblong.

Mouth swollen — who can bear it — can you bear it can you
bare it — the familial blue

extravagant shudder? It is spring.
Wake up Wake up and still spring, and the goats

they bleat *Hariklea, Andreas, Sultana, Ourania, Nausicaa*
and from my basil bowl too

the bones resembling

say it
Katerina
        Yes. and yes.

Me of Me

My namesake wears my heart.
I swim the quarry back and forth.
My face carries my weight
like a prayer nailed half-mast to a flagpole.
It's blowing *Trapezítsa*
where *Katerína* reaches the stars.
The mouths of the villagers sing in smoke.

Notes

p. 9 "Seed," inspired by Eavan Boland's poem "Lava Cameo."
- Amygdaliés is a village in northcentral Greece where Hariklea Papacristou Bargas Samaras, my maternal grandmother was born.

p. 11 "Kaliméra, Kaliméra," *Kaliméra* Good Morning in Greek; *Katerina* is the Greek form of Katherine/Catherine.

p. 12 "vein," *paximathia* is a traditional Greek cookie; Trapezítsa, village in northcentral Greece where Andreas Samaras, my grandfather was born.

p. 14 "For Sacred Purposes: The Boy, the Herd, the Gold," *khrysos* gold;
- Goat herds are hierarchical and are led by females.

p. 15 "Koύkla," doll or young girl in Greek.

p. 16 "Filigree," is for my daughter, Dimitra Schreiber.

p. 17 "Braid," *psomi* bread in Greek language.

p. 18 "Grevenά People," Grevenά a town and municipality in Western Macedonia, Northern Greece where my maternal grandmother, Hariklea Papacristou Bargas Samaras was born in the village of Amygdaliés.

p. 19 "*The Soup, Margiritsa*," is for my mother, Nancy Strisik/Nausicaa Sultana Samaras;
- *basil breeze* Odysseus Elytis "Anoint the Ariston," *The Little Mariner*, Copper Canyon Press, Washington 1988.
- *Margiritsa* is eaten to break the fast of the Greek Orthodox Lent consisting of the offal removed from the lamb before roasting, flavored with seasonings and sauces.

p. 21 "Fried Eggplant Sandwiches," *Pappoús* is grandfather and *Thia* is aunt in Greek language.

p. 23 "With Panagia," (all holy) is for Pamela Giannatsis, dear friend from childhood: Amygdaliés and Trapezitsa are villages in northwestern Greece; Yiayia and Pappoús (grandmother and grandfather); Ahépa (American Hellenic Educational Progressive Association); feta (brined curd white cheese); psomi (bread); katsiróla (pan/pot); finikia, Greek pastry; dolmáthes, stuffed grape leaves; stóma, mouth; thia, aunt; thio, uncle; kouzini (kitchen); foúrnos (oven); mousakás (eggplant casserole); spanikópeta (spinach and feta pie); prása (leek); chórta (wild greens).

p. 24 "Hariklea," ancient Greek name meaning great glory and elegance.

p. 25 "Centuries Old Kako Mati," evil eye.

p. 28 "27 Romanou," is for Mathew Halpin, Director/Founder of Lakkos Artist Residency, Heraklion, Crete.

p. 29 "Labyrinth," Fortetsa is a Settlement in Heraklion, Crete, Greece.

p. 32 "Cretan Olive Oil," *aromatiko'* means aromatic.

p. 33 "*kalispera*," good afternoon in Greek;
- *pure and familiar silence* – inspired by Jane Hirshfield's poem, "This Was Once a Love Poem," Given Sugar, Given Salt, Perennial 2002.

p. 36 "Taverna Zaxaris at Paleokastro Beach," *fy'-ge* means get away in Greek language.

p. 38 “The Sea,” *in the light/the moon sends back* – from Galway Kinnell’s poem, “Little Sleep’s-Head Sprouting Hair in the Moonlight,” *The Book of Nightmares*, Houghton Mifflin Company, Boston 1971.

p. 40 “Goddess to Goddess,” *opa* is a Greek expression/utterance often used in the celebration of life when dancing and/or singing; *agape* is the Greek word for love; *Kríti* is Crete.
- inspired by Tommy Archuleta’s “Vision after vision,” *Susto*, The Center for Literary Publishing, Colorado State University, Fort Collins 2023.

p. 41 “Agora,” a gathering place/marketplace;
- *must chew gently* Natasha Sajé “Game,” *Red Under the Skin*, University of Pittsburg Press, Pittsburg 1994.

p. 42 “After Playing Für Elise,” is for Sarah Kafatou.

p. 45 “Goat, Goddess, Moon” is for Aretusa Leronymaki.

p. 46 “Dawning,” inspired by Constantine Cavafy’s poem “Comes to Rest.”
- *become incapable of caution* from Constantine Cavafi’s poem “Comes to Rest.”

p. 49 “Sefer,” is rooted in the Arabic word for journey;
- *O Heraklion,/this is about/ myself. Adrift.* - influenced by Charles Simic’s poem “Romantic Sonnet,” *Hotel Insomnia*, Harcourt Brace Jovanovich, Orlando 1992.
- Archanes is a rural settlement having deep roots in Minoan antiquity on the outskirts of Heraklion, Crete.

p. 51 “Humid Weather,” after Lucie Brock-Broido “In Owl Weather,” *Stay Illusion*, Knopf, New York 2013;
- Lakkos is a neighborhood in Heraklion, Crete that was once the underground district.

p. 54 “Aikaterina,” (Ai/ka/te/ri/na) is the ancient Greek form of Katherine/Catherine;
- many lines inspired in the knowing of B.C.

p. 64 “White Orchid,” inspired by Kevin Young’s poem “Pity,” *Book of Hours*, Knopf, New York 2014.
- *Finikia* is a honey-flavored traditional Greek pastry.

p. 66 “Ceremony: A Kind of Greek Woman,” is for Anastasia Papageorgiou.

p. 67 “Bone Cavity,” lists the names in Greek of deceased family members, *Hariklea, Andreas, Sultana, Ourania,* but for one *Nausicaa,* my still living mother.

p. 68 “Me of Me,” from Kimberly Johnson's poem “Whiskey,” *Uncommon Prayer*, Persea Books, New York 2014.

About the Author

Catherine Strisik, poet, teacher, editor is the author of two other poetry collections, *The Mistress* (3: A Taos Press) and *Thousand-Cricket Song* (Plain View Press), and chapbook *Insectum Gravitis* (Main Street Rag). Her honors include a New Mexico/Arizona Book Award and finalist citations for the Philip Levine Book Award, Two Sylvia's Press Book Award, Elixir Press Book Award, and New Mexico/Arizona Book Award. She is publisher and editor of *Taos Journal of Poetry,* former poet laureate of Taos, New Mexico, as well as the recipient of a Taoseña Award as Woman of Impact for her many decades of literary contribution in northern N.M. Strisik is a Pushcart nominee with over 30 years of publications with poetry translated into Greek, Persian, and Bulgarian. Currently she divides her time between Cape Ann, MA and Taos, N.M. offering editorial consultations for essayists and poets and facilitates both private and small group poetry workshops. Strisik is a retired dyslexia language therapist.

www.cathystrisik.com